What people are saying

I've heard it said the church is not supposed to be a museum for the saints but a hospital for sinners. If that's true, prayer should not be a performance by the pious but a cry from the broken.

Jesus is a person of authenticity. Jesus wept. Jesus cried out. Jesus welcomed the hurting. Jesus said, "come to me all were weary and burdened." Jesus said to "let the little children come to me." He said, "come to me all who are thirsty."

In *Don't You Care That We Are Drowning?,* Brian Spahr shares the real-life stories and prayers of people crying out in the way Jesus describes. His authenticity helps usher the broken-hearted into the presence of Jesus. This book connects with the deepest part of our hearts. It is a must read.

Bob Lenz
President and Founder of Life Promotions, Appleton, WI

This book is beautiful. My heart broke a million times again and again, as the stories of loss cut closely to my own. It helped me think about God in the darkness and God in those times when things are terrible. That God just might be loving us and holding us despite our anger and our grief. God might just be understanding us when we don't understand ourselves.

Tami-Lewis Ahrendt,
Chief Operating Officer at CenterPointe, Inc., Lincoln, NE

Too many people think of prayer the way they think of writing poetry; some people can do it, the rest of us aren't any good at it. But what if prayer is something that reveals our deepest longings and fears? What if it is a window into our hearts? This book, *Don't You Care That We Are Drowning?*, examines prayers that peer into our hearts and reveal our deepest longings and fears. Like he does in his daily work, through these words Brian sits with us, revealing through his caring presence that, even in life's toughest moments, God is indeed with you.

Dan Bellinger,
Hospital Chaplain, Fort Wayne, IN

Throughout the journey that Brian takes us on in *Don't You Care That We Are Drowning?*, I couldn't help but care - in a more profound way than I ever knew was possible. As he points out, grief is unavoidable; yet there is an unexpected way through. Prayers we weren't taught in church, or even were told "don't count" oftentimes matter more than memorized words can convey. Brian shares powerful stories of people in grief, and the comfort that comes from knowing there is permission to breathe fresh air and speak fresh words. This book has never been more needed.

Beth Fisher,
Speaker and Author of Remorseless

To find a person who lives compassionately is the essence of charity. To be led and guided by one who repeatedly demonstrates a conviction and commitment to faith and truth is the stuff of nobility and integrity. To find a blend of these things in one individual is a rarity. Brian Spahr is that rare individual.

His stories entwined with his faithfulness wrapped up in deep care and love for others, all covered over with an unflagging faith in our loving Savior, Jesus, draw us not only to the heart of Brian but to the heart of the Gospel. His stories and encouragement from his vulnerability do not betray a weakness but instead demonstrate a profound strength in which we can see and use to carry on in our own lives. Brian offers gentle but persuasive wisdom to help us keep our footing when the path gets slippery and the vision is cloudy. Brian's messages are indeed like an arm around the shoulder as we make our way onward.

Pastor Bill Yonker,
Senior Pastor, Immanuel Lutheran Church of East Dundee,
IL

People are often confused by prayer. They are convinced that there is a "right way" to talk to God or that only certain people can pray "the right way". From that perspective, prayer not only seems overwhelming but even becomes a burden. In *Don't You Care That We Are Drowning?*, Brian gets to the heart of the matter and provides readers with a realistic perspective of prayer. He speaks to the desperation we feel in calamitous moments and liberates us from any formal or obligatory prayer format. Brian helps us recognize our everyday pleas in everyday language are truly prayers to God. His reflections are genuine and relatable for all praying people. Thank you, Brian, for letting the Spirit guide you in such a time as this.

Rev. Tim Graham,
Senior Pastor, Messiah Lutheran Church, Fort Wayne, IN

We have all said it, thought it, or felt it at one time or another. "Don't you (or anyone) care that we are (I am) drowning?" If I am honest, I have thought about it in the past week while taking care of my Mom after suffering a stroke. Oh, how life can change in a minute. With refreshing transparency, Chaplain Brian Spahr reassures us that while it is normal to sometimes feel this way, we most definitely are cared for and are not alone during life's struggles, sufferings, and unwanted moments. Through his personal experience, Brian shares vignettes and spiritual truths in *Don't You Care That We Are Drowning?* likely to bring tears to your eyes, comfort to your griefs, and "care" to your soul.

Jane Munk, MA, MBA
Founder, Kerith Brook Retreats for Grieving Adults
Coach, Counselor, Chaplain

Simply put, this book is a gift.

It is said that the final stage of grief is not acceptance but finding meaning. How can humans possibly make meaning out of loss and use tragedy for good? Through profound stories of gut-wrenching loss, *Don't You Care That We Are Drowning?* acts as a much-needed guide showing us the way forward. And that way is authenticity.

Few books I've read have made me stop, set down the book, and pray. And I mean truly pray. Then, pick it back up and read it very slowly so as not to miss the holy gravity of what was being shared. This book is one of those. It's an invitation into the heart of God. And it reveals that God's heart has been with us all along. In the midst of traumatic loss and the confusion, suffering, and hopelessness that accompanies it, these words remind us that we are never alone. And although we may feel numb, or perhaps even hostile, we are actively being loved by the creator of the universe. And, yes, this God cares that we are drowning.

Cody Hardley
Spiritual Director, Fort Wayne, IN

Brian Spahr is the pastor we all need right now and *Don't You Care That We Are Drowning?* is the prayerbook we all need right now. With the heart of a chaplain, the soul of a mystic, and the words of a songwriter, Brian crafts stories that invite us to notice how our hearts are already praying to God in our lament, our anger, our disappointment, our heartache, and in our drowning. These prayers drip with reality, brokenness, hope, and healing.

Jeremy Myers
Associate Professor of Theology and Public Leadership, Augsburg University, Minneapolis, MN

I've been a chaplaincy leader for nearly a decade. Dozens of professional chaplains have served under my leadership. With help from others, I have conducted more than 300 interviews. I have hired chaplains. I have fired chaplains. I've seen chaplains work miracles, have their hearts broken, and walk into rooms where angels fear to tread. During my tenure, our team has responded to more than 10,000 patient deaths. Ten. Thousand. Deaths.

It's possible that I know, better than anyone else, what it takes to be a great hospital chaplain.

And, if I built a prototype for future chaplains, I could start with Rev. Brian Spahr. He is tenderhearted yet tenacious. Compassionate and calm. Warm and spiritual. But most of all, he is loving and honest. If you read *Don't You Care That We Are Drowning?*, you know exactly what I mean. Thank you, Brian, for putting into words the ineffable realities of life, death, grief, and God.

Patrick Riecke
Director, Dignity and Spiritual Care
Parkview Health

"Don't You Care That We Are Drowning?"

and Other Unexpected Prayers

Brian Spahr

Peace be with you!

Copyright © 2022 by Brian Spahr.

All rights reserved.

No portion of this book may be reproduced in any form without written permission from the publisher or author, except as permitted by U.S. copyright law.

Scripture quotations marked NRSV are from New Revised Standard Version Bible, copyright © 1989 National Council of the Churches of Christ in the United States of America. Used by permission. All rights reserved worldwide.

Scripture quotations marked CEB from the COMMON ENGLISH BIBLE. © Copyright 2011 COMMON ENGLISH BIBLE. All rights reserved. Used by permission. (www.CommonEnglishBible.com).

Scripture quotations marked MSG are taken from THE MESSAGE, copyright © 1993, 2002, 2018 by Eugene H. Peterson. Used by permission of NavPress, represented by Tyndale House Publishers. All rights reserved.

Contents

FOREWORD	1
INTRODUCTION	3
A PRAYER TO START	9
1. YOU DON'T KNOW	11
2. THIS SUCKS	13
3. PLEASE, GOD. NO!	16
4. WHAT DO WE DO NOW?	19
5. THIS IS YOUR CHILD	22
6. HOW?	25
7. THE SOUND OF A BROKEN HEART	28
8. SILENCE	31
9. IT'S NOT FAIR	34
10. WHY DON'T YOU DO SOMETHING?	38
CONCLUSION	41
ACKNOWLEDGEMENTS	45

FOREWORD

On July 18, 2018, I got an email from Brian. He said that he was wondering about working with a spiritual director. I had explained that I wasn't one, but that I talk with people and listen and make suggestions.

He wrote, "Would there be an opportunity soon for us to have a conversation and explore the possibilities?" It was the beginning of a relationship that now has us working on the same chaplaincy team. But it is, as I read it again years after he wrote it, an interesting sample of a prayer.

"God, could we talk sometime soon? And you could see if what I'm thinking makes sense?"

It's not demanding; it's not specific about requests. It's a simple openness to talking together. Which is what happens when Brian and I are in the same space and the pager is quiet. We are simply finding out, with God, if what we are thinking makes sense.

+++

I've written a couple collections of prayers that I share every Sunday in the hospital chapel (and online). I try to give words to what people are feeling as we look at the Bible, at the world around us, at our own lives. It's one approach to the work of a pastor. This book of Brian's takes a different approach. Instead of giving people words, Brian looks at the words we speak to and at God and says, "That counts! You are praying!" It is a different work than mine, and often more helpful for the long-term life of a person.

Eugene Peterson was a pastor and writer who has shaped both Brian and me. In Peterson's biography, Winn Collier writes, "Whenever people asked for spiritual guidance, he'd explain that he had few answers, no spiritual techniques—but he could help them learn to pray. Teaching people to pray and teaching them to die a good death—Eugene often said these were the two essentials in the job description of a pastor."[1]

That's been Brian's work as a pastor, and now as a chaplain. I think that it's actually Brian's work as a person. Teaching us to pray and teaching us to die a good death.

It's a good and helpful work. And this book, these unexpected prayers, teach us well.

Rev. Jon Swanson, Ph.D.
Staff Chaplain, Parkview Health
Author, *This Is Hard: What I Say When Loved Ones Die*

---

1. Winn Collier, A Burning in My Bones (Colorado Springs: Waterbrook, 2021), 268.

INTRODUCTION

On January 17, 2019, I had a heart attack. It was a snowy day, and when I arrived at my office, no one had cleared the walks in front of our building. A Bible study group was meeting that morning, and the walks needed to be shoveled. So, I started clearing a path, muttering in frustration under my breath.

"This isn't what I went to seminary for. I don't have a master's degree in building maintenance! My to-do list is already a mile long and this is the last thing I need to be doing right now!!"

As I plowed, frustration became anger. I stomped, and I muttered. But with each stomp and mutter, it got harder to breathe. Something was off. My head started to hurt from the back of my neck to the front of my forehead. But there was still snow on the sidewalks, so I kept going until I finished the job. I couldn't breathe, so I sat down to catch my breath. It never came. A few minutes later, a friend was driving me to the hospital. On the way to the emergency room, I wept in pain and cried out,

"Please God, NO!" and, "WHY IS THIS HAPPENING?!"

I was 49 years old and about to die.

Reflecting on this later, I thought about the story in Mark 4. Jesus was out in the middle of a lake with his friends. We read that "Gale-force winds arose, and waves crashed against the boat so that the boat was swamped. But Jesus was in the rear of the boat, sleeping on a pillow. They woke him up and said, 'Teacher, don't you care that we are drowning?'"

Don't you care that we are drowning?

That desperate cry is now my favorite prayer in the Bible. Maybe it doesn't sound much like a prayer to you. It's nothing like the prayers I prayed in Sunday School or in a lifetime of going to church. It's not how I learned to pray in seminary. But if prayer is an open conversation with God, then "Don't you care that we are drowning?" is exactly the kind of prayer Jesus invites us to pray when we're struggling.

It's honest. There's no pretense. For some reason, we tend to think prayer needs a bunch of big words and flowery language. It doesn't. Say what's on your mind. Talk how you talk. Formal language isn't necessary.

"Please God, no!"
"Why is this happening to me?!"
"Don't you care that we are drowning?"

No, these aren't what you might think of first when you think of prayer. But they are a lot like the honest, irreverent things people say to God throughout the Bible. Like when the writer of Psalms says,

"How long, O Lord? Will you forget me, forever? How long will you hide your face from me? How long must I bear pain in my soul, and have sorrow in my heart all day long? How long shall my enemy be exalted over me?" Psalms 13:1-2 (NRSV)

and,

"My God, My God, why have you forsaken me? Why are you so far from helping me, from the words of my groaning?" Psalms 22:1 (NRSV)

These are just a few examples, but there are plenty of others.

Your prayers won't always need to be so raw. There will be times when your struggle and suffering subside. But when you are neck-deep in pain, I want you to know you can be honest with God about it. You don't have to hold back. There's no need to soften anything. Say what's on your mind. Ask what you need to ask. Jesus wants (and can handle) your honesty. Jesus hears and responds to your honest, raw, desperate, sometimes irreverent, cries. Like when his friends woke him up that day on the boat, asking if he cared.

I work in a job where I often witness God's response to prayers like these. I am a chaplain in a Trauma Center in Fort Wayne, Indiana, where I see awful things every single day. I love my job, but it's hard sometimes. The month before this writing I was with over 30 families as their loved one died or shortly thereafter. I baptized a one-pound baby in the Neonatal Intensive Care Unit minutes before he died. I heard the sound of heartbreak while a mother held her baby son as he took his final breath. I stood in the hallway with a young man as the medical team tried to save his father's life after his heart stopped for no reason. I sat with a woman who made the impossible decision to withdraw treatment and put her mother in hospice care. I sat with families who didn't believe Covid-19 was any kind of threat until their loved one died after that horrible virus destroyed their lungs.

I see awful things all the time. In the halls where I walk, bumper sticker faith, pat spiritual answers, and surface-level prayers don't cut it. Every day I am with people who wonder if God cares that they are drowning, but many of them are afraid to express it.

That's why I'm writing this book. I want to give you (and me and anyone else who needs it) permission to speak freely. There's no need to hold back. If you have something to say to God — no matter how raw and real and irreverent — say it! Pray it!

In this book, I share the real stories and prayers of people who cried out to God amid their struggle and suffering and loss. The prayers are not long or well-spoken. They are things like,

"This sucks." and, "It's not fair."

These are not the kind of prayers you will hear in church, but they are prayers nonetheless. Prayer in its most simple form is talking with God. It is real and raw, and honest, and God is okay with that. God hears and responds to these prayers every bit as much as God does to the more formal, reverent prayers we may be used to. When the disciples prayed, "Don't you care that we are drowning?" Jesus heard them and responded. He stood up (first he woke up, but that's a whole other part of the story) and said to the wind and the waves, "Silence! Be still!" And then, I love how *The Jesus Storybook Bible* says it,

"The wind and the waves recognized Jesus' voice... and they did what he said." [1]

Whether they are reverent and refined, or raw emotion, or even nothing more than a groan, God hears our prayers. And God responds. The wind and the waves sometimes linger on. They don't always immediately subside. But suddenly or subtly, ALL STORMS come to an end and God is still with us. Before, during, and even well after the wind and the waves subside, God is with us!

And that is enough.

When I cried out to God in the middle of my heart attack, there was no immediate calming of the storm, but God was with me nonetheless. The wind and the waves kept raging, but God was there, too. There was no guarantee that everything was going to be okay. The kind of heart attack I had is nicknamed "the widow-maker" for a reason. But the wind and the waves posed no threat to God. I can see that now, and I've made peace with that horrific experience.

God did not leave me alone in my suffering. What kind of loving God would do that? God did not cause my suffering either. I didn't have a heart attack because God was angry with me or because God wanted to teach me something. A God like that wouldn't be worth following. And in my most desperate moments, God didn't give up on me because my prayers were irreverent and raw. Nope. God was, is, and always will be WITH ME! God was listening as I cried out. Eventually, that storm ended, and I found peace. Or maybe peace found me.

The prayers and stories in this book come mostly from conversations I've had with people in the hospital. I've changed some of the details to protect privacy, but every story and prayer is real. I hope you will see yourself in some of them. Maybe some will give you the permission to just use the words and groans you have, even when they don't seem appropriate or enough.

However you pray, whatever you say,

God is listening.
God is with you.
God is speaking to the storms in your life.

And the wind and the waves recognize God's voice.

---

1. Sally Lloyd-Jones, Jago, and David Suchet, The Jesus Storybook Bible: Every Story Whispers His Name, (Grand Rapids: ZonderKidz, 2014), 242.

A PRAYER TO START

"My Lord God, I have no idea where I am going. I do not see the road ahead of me. I cannot know for certain where it will end. Nor do I really know myself, and the fact that I think that I am following your will does not mean that I am actually doing so. But I believe that the desire to please you does in fact please you. And I hope I have that desire in all that I am doing. I hope that I will never do anything apart from that desire. And I know that if I do this you will lead me by the right road, though I may know nothing about it. Therefore will I trust you always, though I may seem to be lost and in the shadow of death. I will not fear, for you are ever with me, and you will never leave me to face my perils alone." Thomas Merton, from *Thoughts in Solitude*

A friend shared this prayer with me a few years ago. Since then I've carried it with me everywhere I go. I love it because most of the time I have no idea where I'm going or what I'm doing. Sure, I make plans and set goals like everyone else. But I never know how things are going to turn out. I never know where life will lead. None of us does. But this prayer helps me remember that it's okay because I'm not alone. I would guess that if you are reading this book, you can relate. So, I invite you to pray this prayer. I invite you to keep it close to you as you wrestle through the pages and prayers ahead. Keep it close, as a reminder that God is with you, even when you have no idea where you are going or what you are doing.

Chapter One

YOU DON'T KNOW

Her wailing pierced through the familiar hum of activity in the Emergency Department. I took a deep breath. I knocked and entered the room to find a woman draped over her husband who had died a few minutes earlier.

"Hi, my name is Brian and I'm one of the chaplains. I'm so sorry…"

Before I could finish she jumped up in a rage shouting,

"YOU DON'T KNOW! YOU DON'T KNOW!" while shaking her finger in my face.

As her shouts returned to wails, she draped herself back over her husband and continued to cry,

"You don't know. You don't know."

I sat down next to her and quietly said,

"You're right. I don't know. I don't know the depth of what you are feeling. I don't know how bad this hurts, but I'm here. If you need to keep yelling at me, that's okay. It doesn't bother me. Let out what you need to let out. I'm here, and I'll stay as long as you need so you don't have to be alone in your hurt.

She fell into me crying,

"You don't know. You don't know."

As her cries softened, I said, "I have no words that will make your hurt go away, but will you try something with me?"

She agreed.

"Let's start by taking one deep breath," I said. "Breathe in and hold it for a few seconds (I'll do it with you) then let it all out."

She took a deep breath, and I said, "That's how you are going to make it through this. One breath at a time."

We sat in that cramped room in the ER and took breath after breath after breath together. All was not made well at that moment. The storm was not stilled. Her loved one was still gone. There was no explanation. But somehow, those deep breaths were holy and sacred. They were hard and healing. She was scared and hurt and felt alone. In her loneliness, hurt, and fear, "You don't know!" was the only prayer she could muster.

How do you pray when you feel alone?

Chapter Two

THIS SUCKS

"I baptize you in the name of the Father, and of the Son, and of the Holy Spirit."

It's normally a joyous occasion when I get to say these words. On this day it wasn't. Baptism feels different when it happens in the Neonatal Intensive Care Unit (NICU). You don't gather around the font in a church building. Instead, you huddle around an isolet, being careful not to knock any lines or monitors loose.

I dipped my gloved finger into a little glass bowl filled with water from the hospital room sink. I reached into the isolet and carefully splashed the drops of water on the forehead of a precious baby boy.

"I baptize you in the name of the Father, and of the Son, and of the Holy Spirit."

He was born almost 4 months premature, and things weren't looking good. I anointed him with oil.

"This child has been sealed with the Holy Spirit and marked with the cross of Christ forever."

A few moments later he took his last breath as his parents looked on in stunned silence. They were devastated. I sat with them for a while. We talked a bit, but we mostly sat in silence. Finally, when the time felt right, I offered my condolences and stood up to leave.

As I started to leave the dad spoke up. He said, "You know what? This sucks!"

He immediately apologized in case I was offended (I wasn't).

I said, "It really does," and sat back down.

He said, "We were supposed to go do something fun with our other son today. Instead, we have to go home and tell him his baby brother died."

I nodded and said, "I know that this is going to be really hard."

"Also, our friends have been telling us everything is going to be okay," he continued. "They've been telling us to trust God and that God has a plan. Well if this is God's plan, then God's plan sucks! I'm sorry if you are offended," (I wasn't) "but that's just how I feel."

I told him there was no need to apologize and said,

"I think this sucks, too. I don't know why stuff like this happens, but I'm pretty sure God agrees with you. So, why don't we just let that be our prayer right now? We don't know what to ask for or what to do. We don't have any answers, so let's just be honest with God and each other. This sucks!"

And we sat there. Silent. And in the suckiness of it all, these broken-hearted parents held their precious boy for the last time. They invited me to hold him, too, and I did. I held that precious baby and cried with his mom and dad. I'm pretty sure God was crying too. It was beautiful and holy. It was sacred and healing... and it sucked.

How do you pray when things suck?

Chapter Three

PLEASE, GOD. NO!

I lay on my side staring at the walls of the tiny, colorless hospital room. The skin on my arm and hand was bruised and irritated where they had placed the IV. Stickers held the wires of a heart monitor on my newly shaved chest. My eyes were wet and blurry. I'd given up trying to fight back the tears. I had a heart attack.

I HAD A HEART ATTACK!

I was 49 years old, and I almost left my family without a husband or a father. That is what was behind my desperate prayer on the way to the hospital. That is why I continued to pray throughout the night,

"Please, God. No!"

The heart attack hurt like hell, but I didn't cry out because of the physical pain. I cried out because I was afraid. I was afraid of what I was about to lose. I was afraid for Michelle if she had to navigate life as a single parent. I was afraid for my kids if they had to grow up without a dad. I was afraid of what my life would look like if there was serious damage to my heart (thankfully there wasn't). I was afraid of all the work that was ahead if I wanted things to be different. So, I lay there in a heap, pleading with God.

"Please, God. No!"

I wish I could tell this story differently. I wish my desperate pleas had transformed into declarations of faith. But that's not how it went.

"Please, God. No!"

That was all I could come up with. Those were my words. Over and over they came to my lips.

Now, I'm not a person who believes you have to beg and plead with God. If God loves us (and God does), and if God is good (and God is) then why would God expect us to beg for what we need? I don't expect my kids to beg me for anything. Why would God?

Thinking back on that night — that long, miserable night — I'm still convinced that God didn't need (or want) me to beg. But somehow my fearful plea became like a centering prayer. In the middle of my fear, it centered me on God's presence right there in the middle of the worst night of my life. As I cried out like a little child, it was like I was resting my head in the lap of the one who created the universe. It was like a loving parent holding me close, inviting me to let it all out.

There was no judgment.

There was no condemnation for what I should have done to avoid being in this situation.

There was no command about what I should do next.

There was only love.

How do you pray when you are afraid?

Chapter Four

WHAT DO WE DO NOW?

"Before you go in, I want to warn you. The dad is cold as ice. He's been super rude to everyone."

A teenage girl had taken her own life, and I was about to walk into the room to meet with her parents. The nurse wanted to make sure I knew what to expect, especially from the father. I knocked and went in. The lights were off, but a little bit of sun still peeked through the drawn curtains. It was enough light to let me see the nightstand beside her bed. There was a picture of the girl. She looked so different. In the picture, she had a bright smile. It was the kind of smile that I could imagine filling even this darkening room. But that smile was gone now, and her parents sat next to her with flat expressions. Tears were not enough for their heartbreak.

I introduced myself and offered my condolences. The mom stared ahead, silent. The dad flatly asked,

"What do we do now?"

When a person dies, one way I can provide care as a chaplain is to help their loved ones identify a practical next step. Deciding on a funeral home and filling out paperwork might seem mundane, but it gives people something meaningful they can do when they have no idea how to move forward. These parents needed those next steps. But despite his flat tone and expression, I had a sense that there was more behind his question. Their light had gone out. The bright smile of the girl in the picture was now just a memory. It wasn't a bulb they could replace or a switch to turn back on. No, this wasn't a pragmatic question (although he struck me as a pragmatist). Their light was gone.

"What do we do now?"

How do you answer that question? What can you say when nothing will make it better? I don't know the right thing to say any more than the next person. But when I face a situation like this, I do my best to remember the way of Jesus. When Jesus went through the towns and villages teaching and healing, he saw many lost people — people who didn't know what to do or where to go. Matthew's gospel describes them as, "So confused and aimless they were like sheep with no shepherd." When Jesus looked at these shepherdless sheep, "his heart broke." So, when this confused and aimless dad asked,

"What do we do now?"

I looked in his eyes and my heart broke. I didn't care if he was rude or flat or cold as ice. My heart broke for him. My heart broke for his wife. My heart broke for the rest of their family. I said something like, "Maybe the next thing to do is go home, and hold your other kids close. Surround yourself with people who will love you well." Then I pointed him to some grief support resources. He nodded and said flatly, "Okay."

There was no great transformation. There were no tears or other expressed emotions. Just, "Okay." But I imagined Jesus looking with compassion into those same expressionless eyes saying,

"What do we do now? I don't know. But, whatever comes next, I love you, and we'll do it together."

How do you pray when you don't know what to do next?

Chapter Five

THIS IS YOUR CHILD

There are a lot of things I don't understand about God. I kind of like it that way. It seems to me that someone as vast and powerful as the creator of the universe, shouldn't be easily understood or explained. I love that God is mysterious. I find the mystery of God comforting, but I often come across things that make no sense. They seem wrong, and I wonder why a loving God allows them to happen.

I was asked to pray outside of her room. This patient was on ECMO. ECMO stands for extracorporeal membrane oxygenation. I don't know what any of those words mean, so I'm thankful we use shorthand. What I do know is ECMO is an incredible machine. It pumps the person's blood outside of their body and oxygenates it so the heart and lungs can rest. The way I understand it, it is a final chance at healing for some of our sickest patients.

I looked through the glass door of her room. It was filled with the lines and tubes and pumps of the ECMO machine. The nurse sat attentively with her. I placed my hand on the glass of her door, took a deep breath, and tried to pray.

Nothing.

No words came.

I watched the woman, lying there. She was completely still except for the subtle tremor of the pumps keeping her alive. The scene looked like something out of a science fiction movie. But outside of that room, she was a wife and mother. She was a daughter and a friend. She was a child of God. This all felt so wrong. She was loved and needed by her family and friends. How did she wind up here? Why couldn't (or why wouldn't) God fix this? I'm drawn to the mystery of God, but not this.

As I stood there with my hand on the glass, my thoughts began to settle. A single phrase repeated in my mind.

"This is your child."

It started with an accusatory tone. Like,

"This is YOUR child. Why don't you do something about this?!"

But as I repeated that phrase again and again under my breath, it became something different.

"This is your child."

The accusation left, and I sensed God's sorrow. I sensed the sorrow of a broken-hearted parent.

"This is God's child."

The woman lying in that hospital bed was God's child. The woman hooked up to all those machines was God's child.

The woman holding onto a narrow ledge between life and death was God's child. And in those moments, I sensed God's sorrow. I sensed God's ache and longing for her to be well.

Could God jump in and heal her?

Would God?

If not, then why not?

I don't know. That part remains a mystery. But what is now more clear to me than ever is the deep love God has for God's children. God longs for us to be well. God hurts when we hurt. God is mysterious and unexplainable, but God is also somehow close and knowable. God is mighty and powerful, but God is also loving and good.

YOU, too, are God's child.

How do you pray when nothing makes sense?

Chapter Six

HOW?

"How? How do I decide what to do?"

She had just left a meeting with her mom's medical team. The outlook was not good and the doctor was recommending hospice. We sat in the chapel together as she asked again,

"How?"

She told me that after meeting with the doctor she didn't know what to do. So, she went for a walk around the hospital.

She said, "I don't know why, but I was walking around and wound up in here. I'm not very religious or anything. I've never prayed in my life. So, I don't know what I'm doing in the chapel. Mom's religious, though. She always went to church. Maybe that's why I'm here. Is it okay that I'm in here?"

"Of course it is," I assured her, gesturing toward the colorful stained glass. "This is a beautiful room in an otherwise sterile-looking hospital. I'm glad you're here.

It's a great place to sit and think. Is it okay if I sit with you for a while?"

She agreed, so we sat. Silent. Until again she said,

"How? How do I make this decision?"

I said, "I know this is hard, but tell me more about what you are struggling with. Sometimes it can help to name it and say it out loud."

Through tears, she said, "If I say I want her to go on hospice, am I saying I want her to die? Because I don't want her to die. But I don't want her to hurt anymore either."

I took a deep breath and said, "It sounds to me like you love your mom. I can't tell you what to do, but my guess is whatever decision you make, you'll make out of love."

"I know," she said quietly. Then she asked, "Will you go to her room with me and pray with her?"

We walked down the hall to her mom's room in the Intensive Care Unit and prayed. I don't remember much of what I said, but before I could say, "Amen" she spoke up. Her voice was quiet and trembling, and she prayed,

"God, please take care of my mama. Amen."

I stood there in silence.

I quit trying to fight back the tears and let them come.

This "not very religious" woman who had never prayed in her life just prayed. It was a holy moment. Then she said, more confident now,

"I think I'm ready to make a decision."

She told the nurse she wanted her mom to go to hospice. I went back to my office, and they put the transfer orders in. She died before they could move her.

When I came back down to meet with the woman I asked, "How do you feel about the decision you made?"

"It was the right one," she said. "She was ready, even if I wasn't."

I often think about those holy moments in that hospital room. I think her prayer started with her question back in the chapel. Before she handed her mom over to God's care, her prayer started with the question, "How?"

Prayer doesn't have to be eloquent or wordy or even religious. Sometimes prayer can be as simple as a one-word question like, "How?"

How do you pray when you face an impossible decision?

Chapter Seven

THE SOUND OF A BROKEN HEART

"The Spirit intercedes for us with sighs too deep for words to express." (a paraphrase of Romans 8:26)

I sat in a tiny church in Rapid City, South Dakota, singing these words along with the congregation. It was a refrain they sang as part of their liturgy during the prayers. It's been over 25 years since that Sunday morning, but those words and that melody still play in my mind on a loop.

+++

We stood in the hallway of the Pediatric Intensive Care Unit. None of us could speak. Her cries—God, I will never forget the sound of her cries.

One of my co-workers said, "That's what a broken heart sounds like."

I'm sure she is right.

They were a mother's cries. Her little boy just died in her arms. No reason. No explanation. He just died. In the hospital, we see a lot of terrible things. We learn to deal

THE SOUND OF A BROKEN HEART   29

with death as part of our job. But none of us ever gets used to seeing kids die. It's beyond explanation, and it leaves deep scars.

I took a deep breath and knocked. I walked into the room, and the grief was suffocating. Nothing I could say or do would help make sense of what happened, so I just looked around the room. I looked into the eyes of the boy's grandparents and friends and aunts and uncles and parents and said, "I'm so sorry." That's all I could say. "I'm so sorry." And I stood there with that beloved family as the mom continued to cry. Her cries were even more piercing now without the buffer of the closed door between us. She cried and rocked her little boy in her arms.

"That's what a broken heart sounds like."

Yes. My co-worker was right. That's the sound.

As we stood there, the words and melody came into my head. That little refrain from Romans 8:26 started to play on its old familiar loop. I asked if it was okay if I prayed. Mom gave me a slight nod between cries, so I did.

I said, "There are no words. I don't know what to say. There's nothing I can say that will make any of this better. This beloved family is hurting beyond description. So, how do we pray at a time like this? I don't know, God. So, I'm going to trust that you do. I pray that you will hear this mother's cries as the prayer that they are. I pray that you will bring her and all of those gathered here reassurance of your love. We need it now more than ever."

And in my head, I sang, "The Spirit intercedes for us with sighs too deep for words to express."

My words were a prayer, but God didn't need my words. God was already listening to the mother's cries. And as we wept together, the Spirit wept with us. God heard and knew and felt our pain. The Spirit interceded for us and God's sighs were even deeper than our own. They were too deep for words to express. God's heart broke with ours.

How do you pray when your heart is broken?

Chapter Eight

SILENCE

"Oh, daddy. I don't even know what to say."

Her voice shook over the speakerphone as she fought back tears. "I'm on my way."

"Please be safe," he replied. "I can't bear to lose you, too."

His wife was hit by a car and died shortly after arriving in the emergency room. I put my hand on his shoulder as he slumped over her body. I said, "I'm so sorry." But nothing else came out. He nodded through his tears but didn't speak. I opened my mouth to say something else, but I stopped myself. I sat down next to him, and his daughter's words played over again in my head. "I don't even know what to say."

"I don't know what to say either," I thought to myself.

"What should I say?" No words came to my lips.

"I should say something, right?" Still nothing.

Silence.

What do you say when there is nothing to say?

So, I didn't say anything. I just stayed there next to him. Silent. Neither of us spoke. After a few minutes, it stopped feeling awkward and started feeling right. He didn't want to be alone, but he also didn't want to talk. He wanted me to stay with him until his daughter arrived, so I did. Sometimes he shook his head and sighed deep sighs while he held her hand.

After a while, his daughter arrived. She fell into his arms and said, "Oh, daddy." They held each other close and cried. No words. Words weren't needed. Words would have gotten in the way. Their silence was their prayer, and God was listening.

Prayer is more than the words we say. Words help sometimes, but they can also be a hindrance. Words can be awkward or even harmful. That day no words would have been more prayerful or honest than our silence. Eventually, they would need to talk, and they did. But for most of the time we sat together in that room, words would have been more disruptive than helpful.

One of my least favorite "Christian" sayings is, "God showed up." I don't like it because it implies that God is usually off somewhere else, doing who knows what. It implies that if we can get God's attention through some kind of activity (i.e., prayer, singing, worship), then God will stop what God has been doing and give us some attention.

I don't like this saying, because God isn't off somewhere aloof and unaware. God is with us! We didn't have to get God's attention that day in the hospital room. We didn't

have to conjure the Holy Spirit with fancy words or a
fervent prayer.

Nope.

God was already there. Where else would the comforter be
other than with God's children in need of comfort? We
didn't have to ask God to show up. God was already there.
As hard and as awful as that situation was, God was there;
and every one of us in the room somehow knew it. When
we finally spoke, that's one of the things they both said,
and I agreed.

Prayer isn't dependent on our words. Sometimes our
silence is the most honest way we can pray.

How do you pray when there is nothing to say?

Chapter Nine

IT'S NOT FAIR

The elevator dinged. She stepped off with purpose, and I was there waiting. I stood up to greet her and broke the difficult news that her mother had died a few minutes before she arrived.

"What? No! What happened? I got here as fast as I could!"

Her mom had a massive stroke and then moved to hospice care, where she had been for two weeks. During that time, her daughter rarely left her side. She would go home each night, long enough to sleep for a few hours and clean up. Then she would return first thing in the morning. But the last few nights were different. It was clear her mom was failing. She camped out in the room, only leaving for a few minutes at a time for food or fresh air.

That night it just got to be too much. She needed to be somewhere else for a while, so she left. It had only been an hour when the nurse called, saying she should return to the hospital right away.

She didn't hesitate. She was on her way as soon as she got the call, but she didn't make it. Her mom died as she

IT'S NOT FAIR

pulled into the parking lot.

I walked her to her mother's room and said, "I'm so sorry."

"I wanted to be here," she replied. "I know it sounds weird, but I wanted to be here."

"It doesn't sound strange at all," I said. "I'm so sorry. I imagine this is hard."

"It's not fair," she said through her tears.

"Tell me about your mom. It sounds like you really loved her."

"That's the thing," she replied. "I barely knew her."

This caught me off guard. I expected a much different kind of reply.

"She walked out on our family when I was little. I tried to keep track of her; but until she had this stroke, I hadn't talked with her in years. It's not fair," she repeated.

I sat with her in silence for a while.

"It's not fair," she said again.

"Will you tell me what isn't fair," I asked?

"Do you mean besides my whole f***ing life!" (Don't be a chaplain if you are easily offended.)

"It's not fair that my mom didn't give a sh** about me! But she didn't give a sh** about me or my brother or anyone else. She left us and our life sucked growing up.

But when she had a stroke, I showed up. And I wanted to be here when she died because her life must have sucked, too. It must have really sucked to be the way she was, and I didn't want her to die alone. Then she died before I got here. Now it feels like one last way she could show me she didn't give a sh** about me or anything I ever needed."

"You're right," I said. "That isn't fair at all. Every kid deserves parents who love them and know how to show it. I'm sorry."

"Yep, but that's my f***ing life."

Her tears were gone now. Her look hardened. Her posture was rigid. The defense mechanism that she thought protected her from the hurtful things in her life had kicked in. That was the end of our conversation.

But her moment of vulnerability stayed with me.

"It's not fair."

Why do some people get such a disproportionate amount of crud to deal with? Why do some people grow up without parents? Why do some people grow up without parents who love them? Why do some people get cancer? Why do some people struggle with mental illness? Why do people get in car accidents? Why do people have massive strokes? Why?

It's not fair.

We've all said it. We've all felt it. Maybe reading this you expect me to offer some kind of explanation or justification. I'm not even going to try. Many of us are conditioned to pretend that everything is okay, even when it's not. I can't tell you how many people going through impossible, unfair things have told me things like,

"It's okay, because God has a plan" or, "It's okay because what Jesus went through on the cross was way worse."

These (and other statements like them) are unhelpful. I would even argue they are toxic. People say them because they seem like good news in tough times, but they aren't.

There is nothing holy or spiritual or religious about hiding behind statements like these. They only belittle us and invalidate our true feelings. Does that sound like something a loving God would want for us?

God is compassionate.
God is loving.
Sometimes life is unfair.

A compassionate, loving God understands that and holds us close when it is.

How do you pray when it's not fair?

Chapter Ten

WHY DON'T YOU DO SOMETHING?

It had been a long few days with little sleep.

We were past the immediate crisis but scared about what would come next. The doctor had been in earlier that day to tell us that our son would be born early... and it could happen anytime.

It was three months too soon.

We weren't ready.
We hadn't read all the books.
We hadn't been to any of the classes.
We weren't even living in our own house.

This was no way to start a family.

It couldn't be time yet. But the doctor said it was. He also said we needed to prepare for the worst. Our son had about a 50% chance of survival, and there would likely be complications if he did.

It was late that same evening. My wife had passed out from a cocktail of stress and medication. I was too exhausted to sleep. I sat on the plastic hospital room couch and stared. I tried to pray, but I couldn't. Finally, I whispered,

"Why don't you do something, God? Why don't you do something!?"

In the background, I heard the soft melody of a worship song playing on a little speaker that sat on the shelf by the window. The singer sang of a mighty God who can move the mountains in a catchy, pop chorus.

I've sanitized this story when I've told it before, but now it's time to come clean. Usually, when I tell this story, I talk about how that worship chorus became the words and melody of my prayer. I talk about how it brought me peace, and how I knew that no matter what happened we'd be okay. I talk about how I got on my knees and prayed. It makes for a good story, but that's not what happened.

Oh, I heard the singer sing his little chorus, but it was like nails on a chalkboard. It wasn't peaceful. It didn't send me to my knees. I wanted to throw the stupid speaker and the stupid song across the room. The chorus grated on my heart and in my ears. It didn't stir my spirit; it churned my stomach as he sang so faithfully about this God who could do amazing things.

All I could think was, "If God CAN move mountains, why did we lose two children before this pregnancy? If God CAN move mountains, why are we sitting in a hospital room hoping our unborn child survives the night? If God CAN move mountains, why do I have to anguish this way? Why do I have to anguish over the physical and psychological toll losing another child will have on my wife? On me?"

I didn't know what would happen.

I had no idea if my son would live or die.

I had no idea what kind of complications he would have in life. I was drowning in questions, and doubt, and fear, and anger, and unbelief.

Did God even care?!

I believed God could do something, I just wasn't convinced God WOULD do something.

"Don't you care that I am drowning?"

I looked at my wife, resting in the hospital bed. She looked tired but strong. I got on the floor, but I wasn't on my knees. No. I lay in a heap on the cold floor of that hospital room and wept.

"Why don't you do something? Why won't you do something?"

A few hours later she delivered our baby boy by emergency c-section. He spent the next eight weeks in the hospital. He's now 14-years-old. He's thriving. He's full of life and love.

It turns out that the singer of that grating little chorus was right. God CAN move the mountains. And this time God did.

How do you pray when you wonder if God cares?

CONCLUSION

In 1663, Rembrandt painted "The Storm on the Sea of Galilee." It is a stunning depiction of the storm story from Mark 4. It shows the disciples fighting to keep the boat afloat in the heavy storm. The sail rips in the raging wind. The boat nearly capsizes as waves crash against the hull. A few of the disciples are praying with their heads bowed. One disciple is throwing up over the edge. Others are fighting with the sail. Some are stirring Jesus awake, pleading,

"Don't you care that we are drowning?"

The newly awakened Jesus' facial expression remains calm and peaceful.

The original painting was stolen in a massive art heist in 1990 and has never been recovered. Thankfully, there are countless re-creations; and scans of the original are easy to find on the internet, so the image isn't lost completely.

There are so many striking parts of this painting, but one detail grabs my attention the most. In the bottom center, one of the disciples is staring directly back at the viewer.

That disciple is Rembrandt himself. Rembrandt painted 13 disciples instead of 12 in his depiction of the storm on the sea. Along with Peter, James, John, and all the rest, he painted himself into the middle of the storm.

There are so many other stories of Jesus in the gospels—happier stories. Why didn't Rembrandt paint himself into one of those? I would have painted myself into the wedding feast. Remember when Jesus turned basins of water into the best wine anyone ever tasted? That sounds much more fun! Or what about the all-you-can-eat bread and fish buffet at the feeding of the 5,000? That would be way better.

But most of life isn't amazing wine and fish buffets. Those times are great when they happen, but it's the storms that shape us. The wind and the waves leave scars and can still drown us long after they subside.

After Jesus spoke peace to the storm in the story, he asked his friends, "Why are you afraid? Have you still no faith?" (Mark 4:40 NRSV)

How we hear this question matters.

When my kids are frightened in a thunderstorm I don't say things like,

"Idiots! Just grow up and don't be afraid!"
"Quit being cowards!"
"Toughen up!"

Instead, I hold them close and tell them how much I love them.

CONCLUSION

I remind them they've heard thunder before.
I remind them they've been through other storms.
I remind them they are not alone.

God is loving and kind. God doesn't chastise us for our fear or our hurt or our sorrow. God isn't a cosmic abusive parent set on belittling and punishing us every time our faith waivers.

God is love.

So, when Jesus asks, "Why are you afraid? Have you still no faith?", I hear it similar to the way I offer comfort and instruction to my kids when they are afraid. In love. With patience and understanding. What if we heard Jesus ask this more like,

"You're afraid. Why? Tell me about it."
"I'm with you."
"You can trust me. Do you?"
"I love you."

The disciples cried out to Jesus in the storm. We cry out to God in our storms,

"Don't you care that we are drowning?"

The answer is, "Yes!"

Yes, Jesus cares that we are drowning. Jesus cares so much that Jesus gets in the boat with us and stays with us even when the wind and the waves are at their worst. Jesus hurts with us and groans with us. Jesus weeps with us and sits silently with us. Jesus speaks to the wind and the waves, and they listen and obey. Jesus stays with us long after the storm ends when there is nothing left but the scars and painful memories. Jesus even takes on the pain and weight of our scars as his own.

That's what a loving God does.

Rembrandt was right to paint himself into the storm.

Where else would he want to be, other than with Jesus, no matter the circumstance?

Where else would we want to be?

"Who then is this, that even the wind and the sea obey him?" (Mark 4:41 NRSV)

ACKNOWLEDGEMENTS

During a Sunday morning shift at the hospital I mentioned the idea for this book to Jon Swanson. His immediate response was, "Sounds good. When are you going to write it?"

The pager was quiet so I said, "I'm going to go in the other room and jot down a few ideas now."

About an hour later I emailed him the first draft of the introduction. He read it and said, "Great! When are you going to finish writing the book?"

I laughed out loud and said, "Well, I hadn't thought that far ahead."

Then I quickly resolved that I would have the first draft finished by the end of December. It was already December. What was I thinking?! But somehow it got done and this book is a real thing that you can read and hold in your hands.

Thank you, Jon, for the prompting and the editing and most of all for your friendship.

Thank you, Nancy and Hope, for reading and editing and helping me refine things as well.

Thank you to the family members and friends who read the original draft, and for encouraging me with your heartfelt comments.

Thank you to the team of chaplains I work with and my leaders at the hospital. I watch you do amazing things every day. You inspire me more than I can express.

Thank you to our patients and families for allowing me to share such sacred space with you.

Finally, thank you to Michelle and Zachary and Marin. I'm so glad we get to be a family. I love you beyond words.

Brian

January 17, 2022
Fort Wayne, Indiana
on the third anniversary of chapter 3.

Made in the USA
Columbia, SC
28 February 2022